Brilliant Bodies

Teeth

By Robin Twiddy

KidHaven Publishing

Published in 2023 by
KidHaven Publishing, an Imprint of Greenhaven Publishing, LLC
2544 Clinton St., Buffalo, NY 14224

Written by: Robin Twiddy
Edited by: William Anthony
Designed by: Danielle Rippengill
Image Credits: All images are courtesy of Shutterstock.com, unless otherwise specified. With thanks to Getty Images, Thinkstock Photo and iStockphoto. Front Cover - Talirina, s_maria, Idol Design, TY Lim, fizkes, didesign021. Images used on every page - Talirina, s_maria, Idol Design. 2 - metsi. 4&5 - GagliardiPhotography, 3445128471. 6&7 - Sharomka, ucchie79, IKO-studio. 8&9 - metsi. 10&11 - TheFarAwayKingdom, Tatevosian Yana. 12&13 - wavebreakmedia, Oksana Kuzmina. 14&15 - KK Tan, Nina Buday, SofotoCool. 16&17 - Dotted Yeti, Alyson W. Kast. 18&19 - Astrid Gast, Sharon Morris, SteffenTravel, Natalia7, EcoPrint, fon thachakul. 20&21 - Gabi Siebenhuehner, Here, bedya. 22&23 - Sudowoodo. 24 - metsi

Cataloging-in-Publication Data

Names: Twiddy, Robin.
Title: Teeth / Robin Twiddy.
Description: New York : KidHaven Publishing, 2023. | Series: Brilliant bodies |
Identifiers: ISBN 9781534542983 (pbk.) | ISBN 9781534543003 (library bound) | ISBN 9781534543010 (ebook)
Subjects: LCSH: Teeth--Juvenile literature. | Human physiology--Juvenile literature. | Human body--Juvenile literature.
Classification: LCC QL858.T835 2023 | DDC 599.9'43--dc23

Manufactured in the United States of America

CPSIA compliance information: Batch #CWKH23: For further information contact Greenhaven Publishing LLC at 1-844-317-7404.

Please visit our website, www.greenhavenpublishing.com.
For a free color catalog of all our high-quality books, call toll free 1-844-317-7404 or fax 1-844-317-7405.

Find us on

Contents

Bodies Are Brilliant

Bodies come in all different shapes and sizes. They are all brilliant!

All brilliant bodies have brilliant parts. One of the brilliant parts of your body is your teeth.

What Are Teeth?

We can find our teeth in our mouths. They cut and chomp and chew.

We use our teeth when we eat. We even use them when we talk. Teeth are brilliant!

Types of Teeth

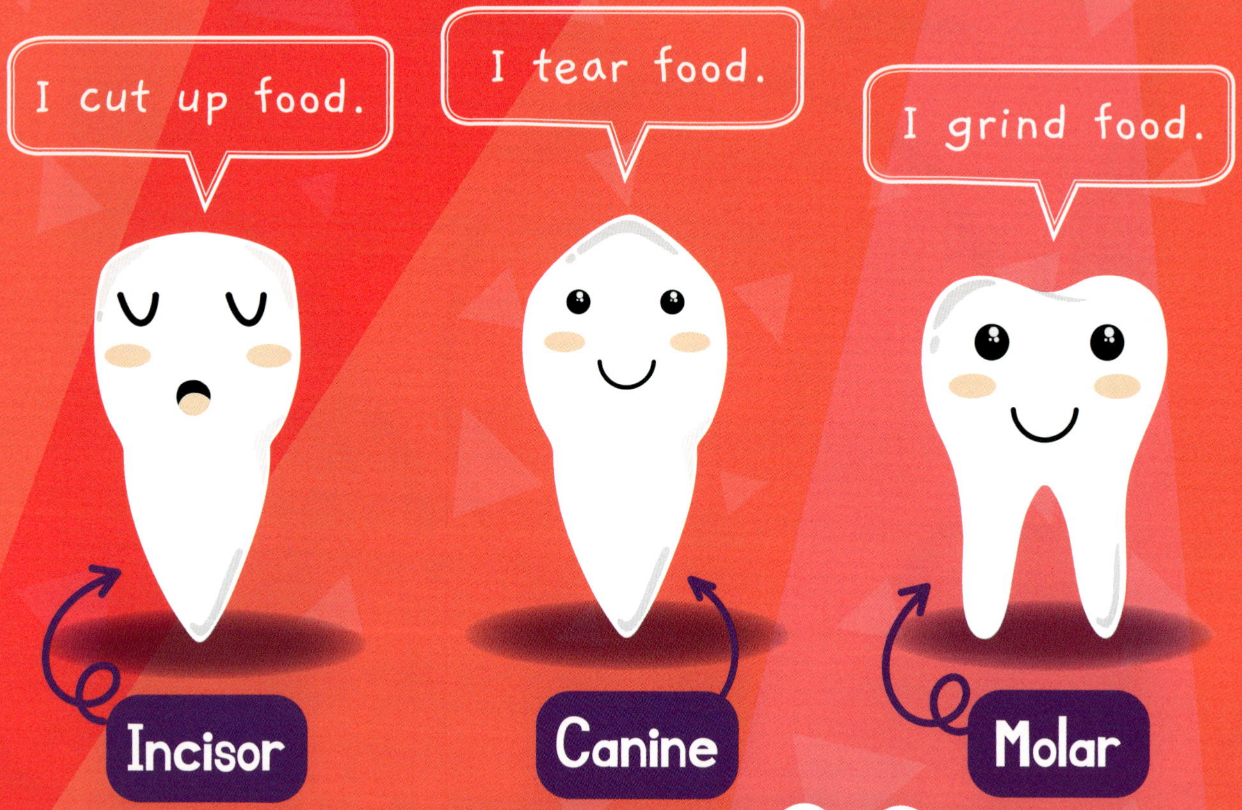

We have three different types of teeth in our mouths.

Each type of tooth has a different job when we eat.

I am using my incisors to bite into this apple.

Which Teeth Where?

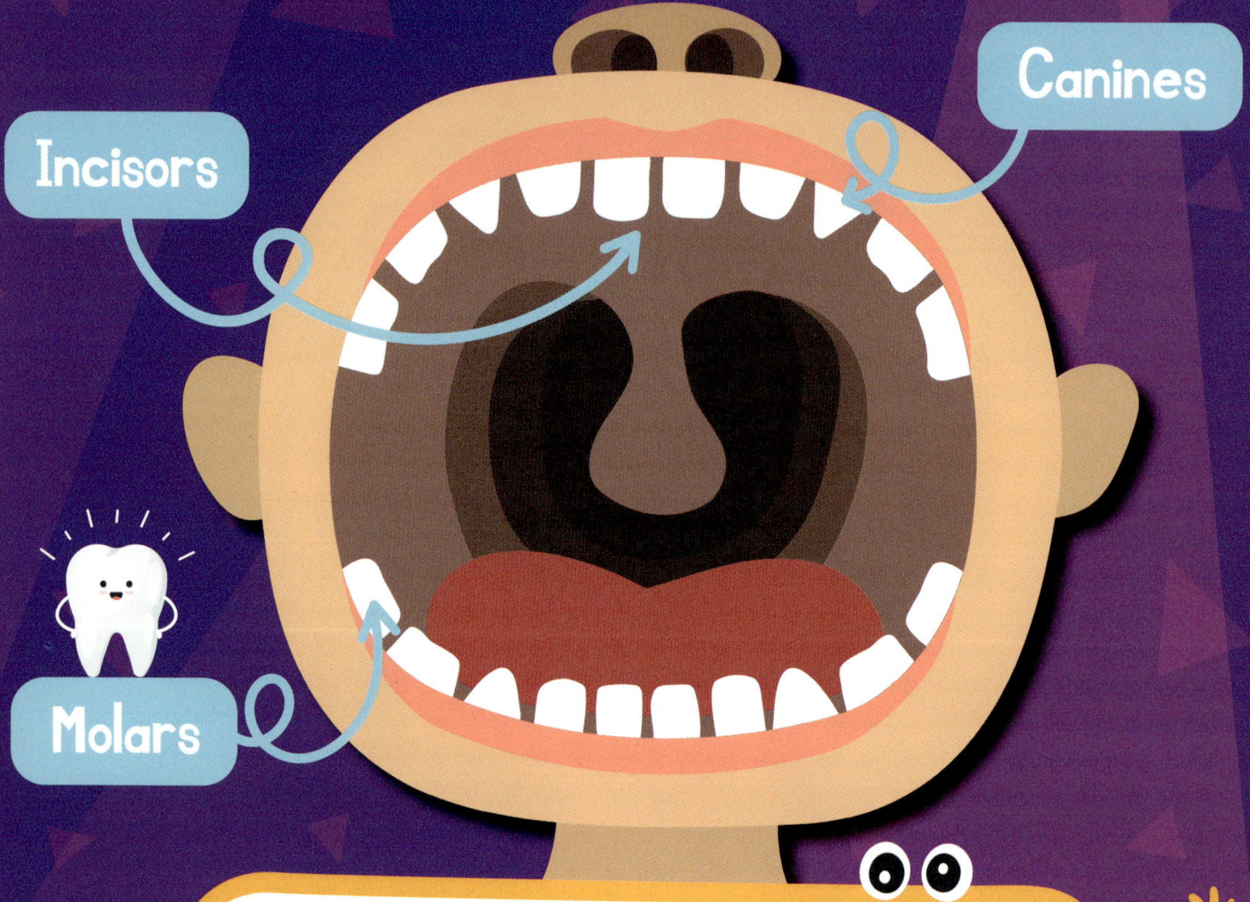

The different types of teeth sit in different places in our mouths.

The teeth at the back of our mouths chew food. The teeth at the front cut and tear food.

Taking Care of Teeth

It is very important to take care of our teeth.

Always brush your teeth before going to bed.

Make sure that you brush your teeth twice a day. You should brush for about two minutes each time.

More than One Set?

Humans have two sets of teeth! As we get older, our first set falls out one by one.

This makes room for our adult teeth.

Some animals have more than two sets of teeth, such as sharks.

Animal Teeth

Lots of animals have teeth.
Some are small and some are big.

Animals that eat leaves and grass often have flat teeth.

Horses have flat teeth to chomp grass.

Cats chew grass to clean their teeth.

Chimpanzee teeth are a lot like human teeth.

Lions have long canines.

Hamster teeth never stop growing.

Elephant tusks are actually teeth!

Hippopotamuses have the longest canines of all animals.

Smiles

Smiling is a brilliant way to show off your brilliant teeth.

We smile when we are happy.

Make sure to visit the dentist to keep your smile healthy.

Brilliant Bits of Bodies

Now we know a little more about our brilliant teeth. Our teeth are just one part of our brilliant bodies!

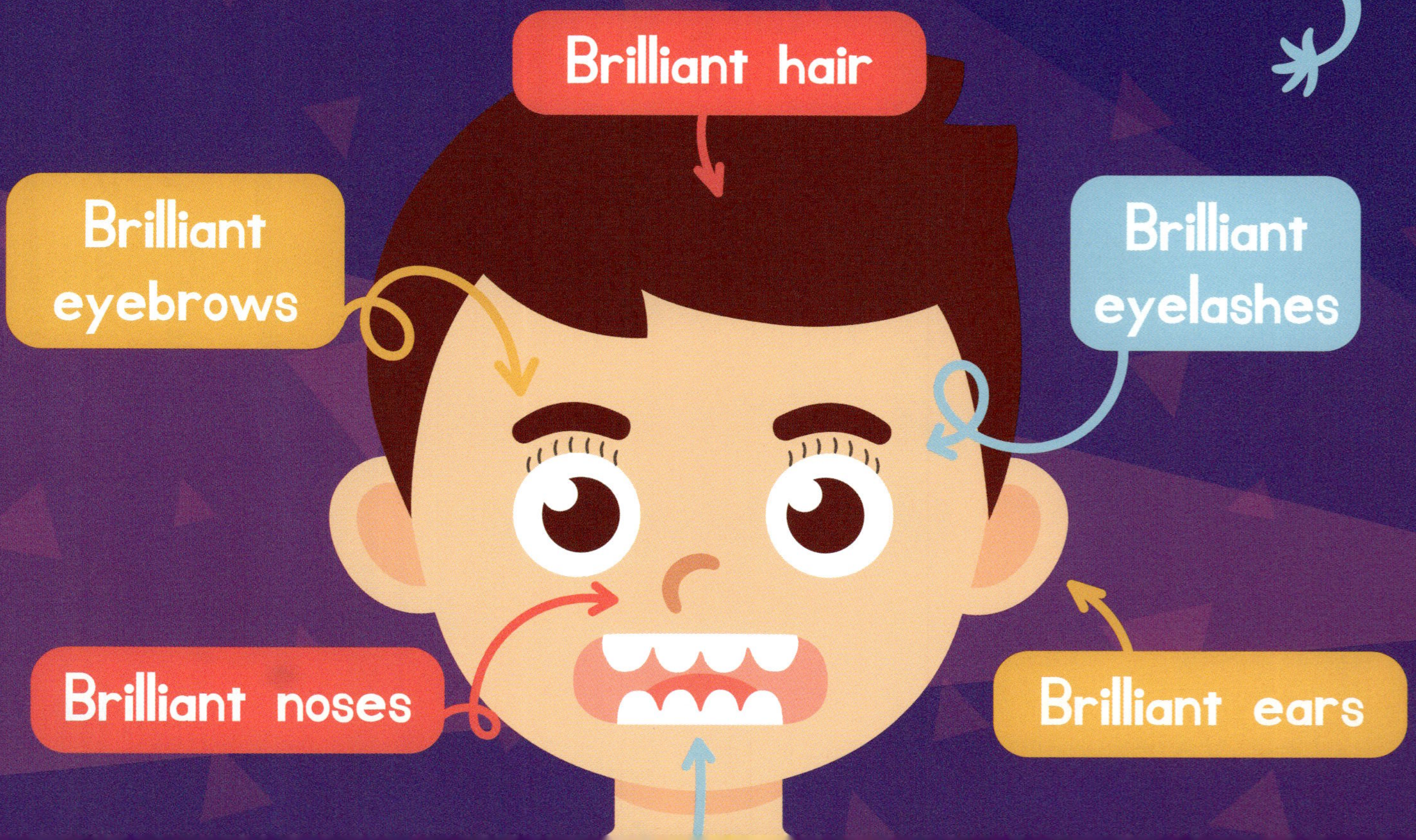

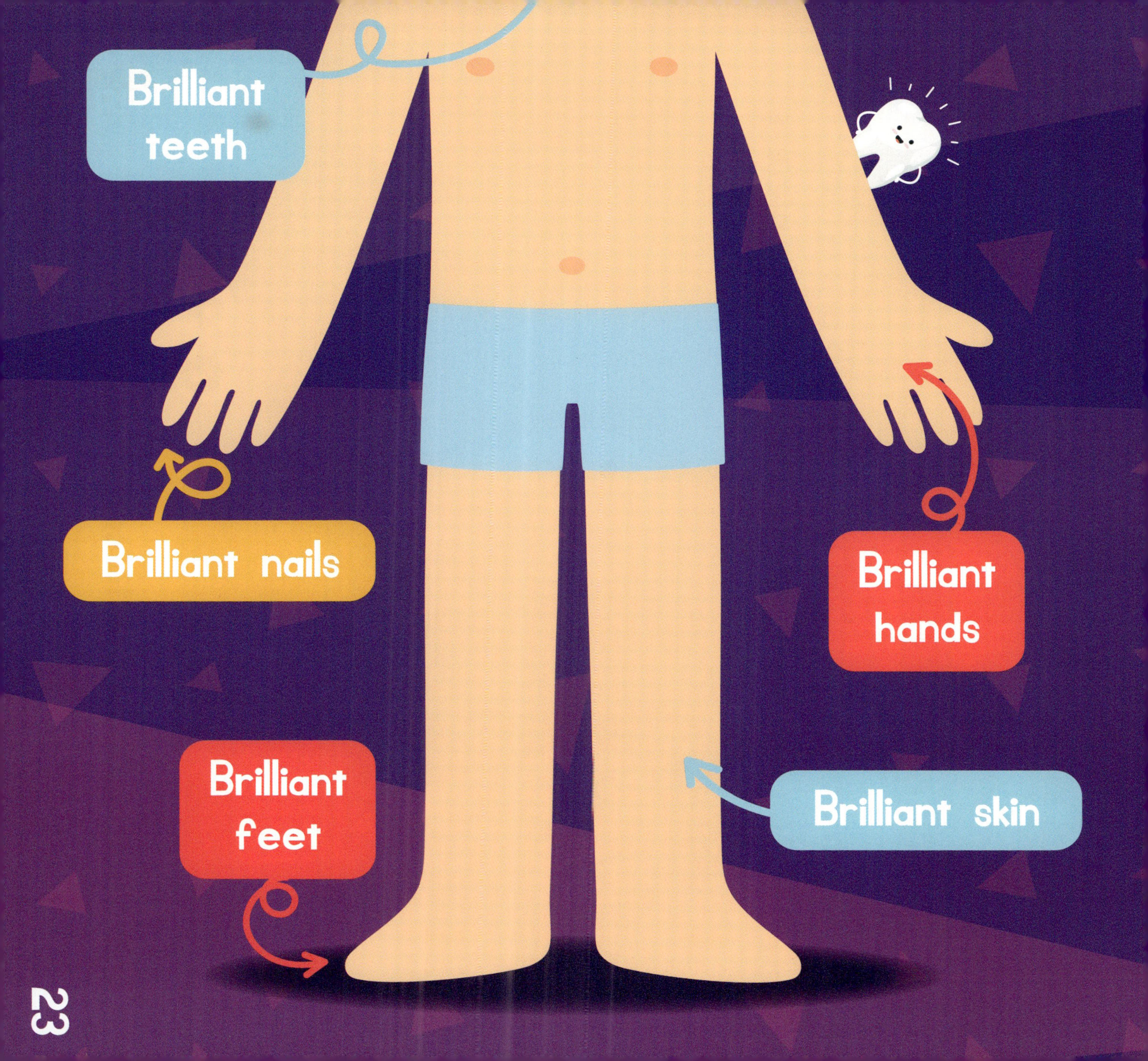
Brilliant teeth
Brilliant nails
Brilliant hands
Brilliant feet
Brilliant skin

Which Teeth?

Can you remember which teeth are which? Match the name of the tooth with its picture.

Check page 8 to see if you are right.